Old Angel Midnight

JACK KEROUAC

OLD ANGEL MIDNIGHT

Edited by Donald Allen

Prefaces by Ann Charters
& Michael McClure

Grey Fox Press
San Francisco

Composition by Harvest Graphics

Cover drawing of Jack Kerouac in 1956
  by Robert LaVigne

Library of Congress Cataloging-in-Publication Data

Kerouac, Jack, 1922-1969.
    Old Angel Midnight / Jack Kerouac ; edited by
Donald Allen : with prefaces by Ann Charters &
Michael McClure.
        p.   cm.
    ISBN 0-912516-97-6 (pbk.)
        1. Beat generation — Poetry.   I. Allen, Donald
Merriam
    II. Title
    PS3521.E735043   1993   93-14684
    811'.54 — dc20   CIP

Distributed by Subterranean Company, PO Box 160,
265 S. 5th St., Monroe, OR 97456 503-847-5274.
Toll-free orders 800-274-7826 FAX 503-847-6018.

Dedicated to
Lucien Carr
the initial inspiration for
Old Angel Midnight

Contents

Ann Charters

"Letting Go" in Writing*

The five notebooks in the Berg Collection (New York Public Library) span the period between 1956 and 1959, important years in Kerouac's literary production, when he had fully matured as a writer. By April 1, 1956, the first date in the notebooks, he had been writing spontaneous prose for five years and was in possession of a highly flexible, original prose style. Before beginning this notebook he had written six novels, a collection of poetry ("San Francisco Blues"), and a book of Buddhist scriptures ("Some of the Dharma). When he began this notebook he was living in a cabin in Mill Valley, California, with the poet Gary Snyder, who shared his interest in Buddhism. It was at Snyder's suggestion that Kerouac began the *Scripture of the Golden Eternity*. . . .

On May 21, 1956, a month after finishing *Golden Eternity*, Kerouac wrote a letter to his friend John Clellon Holmes, telling him about his life in Mill Valley and San Francisco, and complaining, "I don't know what to write any more, I've been finally doodling with an endless automatic writing piece which raves on and on with no direction and no story and surely that wont do tho I'll finish it anyway while doing other things. . . ."

*Excerpted from Ann Charters: "Kerouac's Literary Method and Experiments." *Bulletin of Research in the Humanities*, Winter 1981.

This "endless automatic writing piece" was *Old Angel Midnight*, then titled "Lucien Midnight." Kerouac had begun this poem as an imitation of his friend Lucien Carr's speech patterns in New York the previous year, and it was continued in the pages of the Mill Valley notebook after *Golden Eternity*. It was Kerouac's idea to experiment with free association in this poem, writing down "the sounds of the entire world . . . now swimming thru this window," and he worked on it sporadically for years, conceiving of it as without end or narrative direction. True to his original conception, the lines of "Lucien Midnight" are dispersed throughout all five of the Berg Collection notebooks.

Unlike *Golden Eternity*, there were no revisions in the "automatic writing" entries in the manuscript notebooks, and the poems were transcribed for publication as originally written. Lucien Carr asked Kerouac to change the title of the work from "Lucien Midnight" to the more evocative "Old Angel Midnight," and sections were re-numbered when they were published, but otherwise there were almost no changes. *Old Angel Midnight* was an exercise in pure spontaneous composition. What Kerouac wanted was to chronicle "this inner life which we actually lead, one & all, in the new rhythmic measure which we actually speak, and in the inevitable prose or poetic forms dictated by unique revelation of the mind faithfully notating its own processes." Kerouac had a literary model in the stream-of-consciousness passages in James Joyce's *Ulysses*, but his method was *not* to create a fictional character like

Molly Bloom in whom he could dramatize a human consciousness. Instead Kerouac took his own mind as raw material. His technique of spontaneous prose had its origin specifically in a friend's suggestion that he "sketch" the images of scenes he had witnessed, associating freely with words the way a jazz musician improvised his melodies on a given harmonic structure, but Kerouac's technique of "notating" his own mental processes flowered into its richest, most evocative form after he became interested in Buddhism and meditation.

In his French-Canadian childhood in Lowell, Massachusetts, Kerouac had been raised as a Roman Catholic, and it could be that his later involvement in Buddhism offered not only a new direction for his religious feelings, but also a justification of his decision to write spontaneous prose, since he used meditation techniques to help free his mind for spontaneous composition experiments. Living in Mill Valley with Gary Snyder, who was preparing to study Buddhism in Japan, Kerouac discussed passages from his copy of Dwight Goddard's *Buddhist Bible*, and he tried to emulate Snyder's disciplined schedule of daily meditation sessions. The Buddhist technique of "letting go" was a way that helped free his mind when he worked on *Old Angel Midnight*, annotating the stream of words through his consciousness as he responded to auditory stimuli in his environment.

The different sections of *Old Angel Midnight* in the different manuscript notebooks in the Berg Collection attest to the success of Kerouac's experiment. Often he lit a candle and sat quietly transcribing sounds outside the window before turning within to scribble down his own thoughts and mental images. Since he was making no attempt to tell a story, he wasn't held by any narrative line, so his associations moved freely through thoughts to images to pure sounds to emptiness, where (as in one section in the first Berg notebook) he broke off:

> How are you Mrs Jones?
> Fine Mrs Smith!
> Tit within Tat
> Eye within Tooth
> Bone within Light, like —
> Drop some little beads of
> sweetness in that stew (O
> Phoney Poetry!) — the
> heart of the onion — that
> skin is too good for me
> to eat, you! —
>
> People, schmeople
> (from *Old Angel Midnight 3*)

Old Angel Midnight was a project that helped Kerouac develop his skill at "letting his imagination play" on paper. The pages of the poem in the notebooks bear witness to his commitment as a writer, showing that he practised his method constantly in order to sharpen his imaginative reflexes, and he derived great pleasure from the writing exercise; as he said in *Old Angel Midnight*, "I like the bliss of mind."

Michael McClure

Jack's *Old Angel Midnight*

In the spring of 1956 I was twenty-three years old when I climbed into an old car, with the door tied shut by a piece of rope, and drove across the Golden Gate Bridge to visit Jack Kerouac, who was staying in a shack in Mill Valley. My daughter would be born in a month or so, and I'd just co-edited a literary magazine that had everyone in it from the Black Mountain poets to the anarchists and early Beats. I thought a lot of Jack Kerouac because I saw him as the writer of *Mexico City Blues*, which I'd read in manuscript. When I first met Jack the preceding October, I was impressed with his good looks and self-consciousness; in fact, I thought he might be the only person I'd ever met who was as self-conscious as I was.

The shack was an unfinished house up the slope from Lock McCorkle's home. Mill Valley was only 40 minutes from San Francisco, but it was rural. San Francisco itself, in those days, was a small city, a cow-town/harbortown. McCorkle's shack was in a growth of eucalyptus and some evergreens, and in reading *Old Angel Midnight* again I can almost smell the trees and can easily imagine the rustling and crashing sounds that deer make at night on those hillsides. Often Jack would have sat there by luminous, bright but soft kerosene lamplight, writing away at *Old Angel Midnight*. One of the times I was there Gary Snyder took over our training and had a group of us running single file in the night along trails in the dark, in a Zen running meditation.

Another time I was there it was during the afternoon and there were vultures lazing in circles in the sun over the back roads of Mill Valley, and an occasional red-tailed hawk whistling. I was in the shack thinking of the bareness of it — the wooden floors and absence of windowpanes, and the uncanny stillness. Jack walked outside into a patch of sun in a clearing and read me a little poem about ants "merlying" around. He said the piece was from *Old Angel Midnight* so I asked him what that was, and he replied that it was an unending piece of spontaneous writing he wanted to keep working on till he'd filled a trunk with the pages. I liked the idea of ants merlying — it was the best descriptive word ever for the way they move. Looking down, they were doing that right by our shoes and over the brown earth and between the twigs and leaves.

I see all the faces of one myriad consciousness merlying through this book. Though the voices of *Old Angel Midnight* are often as soft as velvet, there are two rugged chunks of the book, as presented here, butted up against one another. That's the structure. The last part of the book tends to represent itself as an address to *Old Angel Midnight*, and the longer opening section is Jack both being the "Voice" and writing out the "Voice" as it comes through the midnight windows. This willingness to put separate chunks of the same work alongside each other was in the air. The assemblage artists were doing it too. It created a broader field for experience and the reflection of one section in another.

With that said, *Old Angel Midnight* is a pirate's treasure chest. I can sit for a long time running the fingers of my mind through the shining doubloons and emeralds and pull out a crusty necklace of pearls and precious stones draped with sea moss. Anyone who's ever tried to sleep past dawn on a morning while the birds made maddeningly repetitious points on their minds — towhees and black phoebes especially — understands the poem that begins:

> peep
> peep the
> bird tear the
> sad bird drop heart
> the dawn has slung
> her   aw   arrow   drape

This was written while the millions of birds were "yakking" and "barking." Then, in this poem, Kerouac brings in the classical and Shakespearian literary "dawn" by means of a mimicking cadence and a few appropriate words in context. What a pleasure!

Here's an uncut diamond that comes up with my hand as I rustle my mindfingers through *Old Angel Midnight*. Look, it's a haiku:

> Morning sun —
> the purple petals,
> Four have fallen

Section 8 opens with as fine a description of a local landscape as one can imagine: "The Mill Valley trees, the pines with green mint look and there's a tangled eucalyptus hulk stick fallen thru the late sunlight tangle of those needles. . ." I know this is the real thing as I read it — all these beauties in their matrix are glimmering blue-green chunks of striated turquoise seen with their accompanying rock, but there's more to it than that.

Old Angel Midnight refers to the world of memory, and to the universes of dreams and experience, and rapidly melts them all down with spontaneous prose into a plasma, or a soup, of what sounds like "seed syllables." The Hindu gurus believed that the universe of matter had its origin in sounds, and the sounds are called seed syllables. They said everything arose from them and came into being in a net or veil. No matter how vapory such an idea may appear, there is the sense of the absolute real in *Old Angel Midnight*. Jack Kerouac carries such conviction and sense of the truth of what he speaks because by 1956, he'd already written works like *Mexico City Blues*. He had, in addition, made great statements of his sensorium: his eyes, ears, sense of smell, fineness of touch, with accuracy and intimate selfness in novels such as *On The Road*. These books attest to the perceptions of Jack's imagination and nervous system, bound together in the narrative recounting of his life and the lives of his friends. Sometimes this acuteness was in dialog, but mostly it was in the description of events, and of people acting in their personal realities — but, still, Kerouacian prose allowed people to be the spirit lives that they were. Kerouac was prepared to be an athletic and visionary bop prosodist by the spring of 1956.

To get beyond the veil or net of stuff and into touch with onflowing consciousness, it must have made sense to go to something like seed syllables, to a style that was as empty and light and fulfilling in itself as scat singing. *Old Angel Midnight* not only is predicated on Joyce's *Finnegans Wake:* it also feels and sounds much like the milieu from which *Finnegan* arose — from the movement in literature around Eugene Jolas' *Transition* magazine, which printed sections of *Finnegans Wake* serially. The *Transition* movement in art included mystical dadaists and soul-seekers who wanted to give language a "vertical" thrust so that it would rise or plunge toward the Godhead. However, Jack was different: as a Buddhist, he knew that consciousness and "Tathagata"* were always there. He must have guessed that he could become so vulnerable and so permeable to the sound of imagination that he could dissolve into consciousness, into Buddha consciousness and *Old Angel Midnight* consciousness, and especially when the Old Angel was speaking to him through the midnight window of his ears.

---

*Philip Whalen, a longtime friend of Jack's, who is now Abbot Zenshin Ryofu of Issanji Temple, when asked for a definition of "Tathagata," said, "Oh, that's easy: thus come, thus gone; suchness; or, as Suzuki-roshi said, 'Things as is.'"

That definition may be useful to understanding the midnight voice in this book.

When reading the "WAVE" section (9), I see Jack using the whole of his life as experienced through the writing he is doing, in the rapid flow of this Old Angel consciousness, as an instrument of perception. The electron microscope reaching into the molecular innards of cells is an instrument of perception — and so are some poems by Shelley and Su T'ung Po instruments of perception. Kerouac is as radical as an electron microscope, but the word "instrument," which would have appealed to Edgar Allan Poe or Shelley, would not make Jack happy. Let that be.

The bursts of this writing are gems in the matrix of daily life; of drinking sweet red port with friends, of longing for opiates, of deer hoofs trampling the leaves, of car rides and intense conversations and lazy snoozes in the sun. But this writing had to be modest, unpretentious, factual, mystical, yearning, unafraid, serious, comic, easy and inspired.

The WAVE section begins, "Looking over der sports page I see assorted perms written in langosten field hand that wd make the 2 silhouetted movie champeens change their quiet dull dialog to something fog — " Didn't Jack get the "der sports page" from reading the Boer accents in that old-time comic strip *The Katzenjammer Kids*, where the boys, Hans and Fritz, are always playing the brutal prank, and in the end kissing each other in congratulation on the success of their latest wicked scheme? I can see the sports page with its "perms" and I can easily see other comic strips — written in earlier days in a dada lingo: Smokey Stover's "nov shmoz kapop" comes to mind. Jack's view of sports page and the americana of newspaper cartoons leaps right away, for whatever reason, to his insight that "I'm my mother's son and my mother is the universe" — and that speeds one into a poem about wave, then (after an aside) Old Angel continues:

> In a universe of waves quel difference betwixt one wave & t'other? T s all the same wavehood & every little unlocatable electron is a Tathagata pouring electromagnetic gravitational light at the constant speed of light (which can be heard in the sound of silence) & so this endless radiation of mysterious radiance is merely the minutia magnificent endless Tathagata Womb manifesting itself multiply & so not at all, for, all things are no-things but if this bores you it's because you want bricks in your soup. Empty.

As this cartoon strip that Jack is inventing continues, it decides with its own intuition that: "True Nature is incomprehensibly beyond the veil of our senses and is like empty light." In fact, we are moved into a deep and giddy insight regarding the non-physics of Sunyatta emptiness, the Buddhist philosophy of "Nothingness Totality." From there, it is another flick of perception into Jack's wondering why one should fear one's self.

What a unique work *Old Angel Midnight* is. It can be compared to the fourteenth-century English visionary work *The Cloud of Unknowing* as easily as to Krazy Kat. No one but Kerouac can run Ida Graymeadow,

Odin, Loup Gris, the heroes of the Icelandic sagas, Napoleon, "Prick Neon," Buddha and Faust into one long breath of bop prose.

I can't remember anyone but Jack Kerouac who has described the feeling of a cat's lips on his toes: "the little tit tat tadpole honey tweak of kitty lips on my tootsie two toes makes me think of dwiddle tingle tingle springs the ditties of childerhood — " Surely such writing is forbidden in serious gloomy literature as well as to big serious gloomy readers, though I can imagine such words in overlooked pages of Melville.

Number 63 is a short story, a tiny novel, an experience, seen by a man-boy's eyes as he kneels in the sun playfully holding his railroad brakeman's lamp as he looks down on, and participates in, a war of black ants. In his mental eye the sizeless scene of insect carnage becomes an epic science-fiction tale and a planetary vista of awfulness and terror in which, finally, the winged lady ants kick their children out of their miniature floating planets into the endless ant war and voraciousness beneath them. This "story" ends like an ironic passage of the later Mark Twain, it is reminiscent of *The Mysterious Stranger*, as the helmeted ant knight glories over his dying enemy brother, waving his antennae to trumpets of Siegfriedian music.

One could relate *Old Angel Midnight* to Jack' s life and tell why he writes about standing on his head regularly, and who his friend Lucien Carr was — but these things are in the novels, or in biographies. What matters, as I reread this treasure decades later, is the sheer naked inconsequentiality of it.

Never before has inconsequentiality been raised to such a peak that it becomes a breakthrough. The subjective aspects of perception and expression have been pressed against the cloth of that which is daily and ordinary, unto the point where the weave begins to spread and light from another side becomes visible. Inconsequentiality becomes a skewing of the established values of the senses and imagination into strange and yet familiar, but elusive, tantalizing and remarkable, constructs of image and sound. It really is a trembling or a fluttering of what we know as reality. The politics of *Old Angel Midnight* is that it is a reply by Jack to heavily armored, socially approved *literature*, as it was then taught and admired in colleges . . . As it was defined by pipe-smoking tweedy men in libraries, staring into the solemn darkness of the tomes heaped shadowily around their imagined souls.

Old Angel Midnight is contemporary with exploratory jazz and with the painting which sought to make spiritual autobiography utilizing the gestures of the artist and his materials. The need for consequentiality becomes inconsequential, and with this realization, both waves of things and nothingness begin to become visible in the boy-child's play. *Old Angel Midnight* is struggling to be occupied by consciousness and nothingness, and not by social commands. The old values of what was literary or profound come tumbling down in the glimmer of the sometimes smiling, sometimes guilty, and often innocent face that is shining up from the pages.

Old Angel Midnight

1 FRIDAY AFTERNOON IN THE UNIVERSE, in all directions in & out you got your men women dogs children horses pones tics perts parts pans pools palls pails parturiences and petty Thieveries that turn into heavenly Buddha — I know boy what's I talkin about case I made the world & when I made it I no lie & had Old Angel Midnight for my name and concocted up a world so *nothing* you had forever thereafter make believe it's real — but that's alright because now everything'll be alright & we'll soothe the forever boys & girls & before we're thru we'll find a name for this Goddam Golden Eternity & tell a story too — and but d y aver read a story as vast as this that begins Friday Afternoon with workinmen on scaffolds painting white paint & ants merlying in lil black dens & microbes warring in yr kidney & mesaroolies microbing in the innards of mercery & microbe microbes dreaming of the ultimate microbehood which then ultimates outward to the endless vast empty atom which is this imaginary universe, ending nowhere & ne'er e'en born as Bankei well poled when he ferried his mother over the rocks to Twat You Tee and people visit his hut to enquire "What other planet features this?" & he answers "What other planet?" tho the sounds of the entire world are now swimming thru this window from Mrs McCartiola's twandow & Ole Poke's home dronk again & acourse you hear the cats wailing in the wailbar wildbar wartfence moonlight midnight Angel Dolophine immensity Visions of the Tathagata's Seat of Purity & Womb so that here is all this infinite immaterial meadowlike golden ash swimswarming in our enlighten brains & the silence Shh shefallying in our endless ear & still we refuse naked & blank to hear What the Who? the Who? Too What You? will say the diamond boat & Persepine, Recipine, Mill town, Heroine, & Fack matches the silver ages everlasting swarmswallying in a simple broom — and at night ya raise the square white light from your ghost beneath a rootdrinkin tree & Coyote wont hear ya but you'll ward off the inexistency devils just to pass the time away & meanwhile it's timeless to the ends of the last lightyear it might as well be gettin late Friday afternoon where we start so's old Sound can come home when worksa done & drink his beer & tweak his children's eyes —

2   and what talents it takes to bail boats out you'd never flank till flail pipe throwed howdy who was it out the bar of the seven seas and all the Italians of 7th Street in Sausaleety slit sleet with paring knives that were used in the ream kitchens to cut the innards of gizzards out on a board, wa, twa, wow, why, shit, Ow, man, I'm tellin you — Wait — We bait the rat and forget to mark the place and soon Cita comes and eat it and puke out grit — fa yen pas d cas, fa yen pas d case, chanson d idiot, imbecile, vas malade — la sonora de madrigal — but as soon as someone wants to start then the world takes on these new propensities:

   1. Bardoush
      (the way the craydon bi fa shta ma j en vack)

2. Flaki — arrete — interrupted chain saw sting eucalyptus words inside the outside void that good God we cant believe is anything so arsaphallawy any the pranaraja of madore with his bloody arse kegs, shit — go to three.

3 Finally just about the time they put wood to the poets of France & fires broke out recapitulating the capitulation of the continent of Mu located just south of Patch, Part, with his hair askew and wearing goldring ears & Vaseline Hair Oil in his arse ass hole flaunted all the old queers and lecherous cardinals who wrote (write) pious manuals & announced that henceforth he was to be the sole provender provider this side of Kissthat.

Insteada which hey marabuda you son of a betch you cucksucker you hey hang dat board down here I'll go cot you on the Yewneon ya bum ya — lick, lock, lick, lock, mix it for pa-tit a a lamana lacasta reda va da Poo moo koo — la — swinging Friday afternoon in eternity here comes Kee pardawac with long golden robe flowing through the Greek Islands with a Bardic (forgot) with a lard (?) with a marde manual onder his Portugee Tot Sherry Rotgut, singing "Kee ya."

Tried to warn all of you, essence of stuff wont do — God why did you make the world?

Answer: - Because I gwt pokla renamash ta va in ming the atss are you forever with it?

I like the bliss of mind.

Awright I'll call up all the fuckin Gods, right now!

Parya! Arrive! Ya damn hogfuckin lick lip twillerin fish-
monger! Kiss my purple royal ass baboon! Poota!
Whore! You and yr retinues of chariots & fucks!
Devadatta! Angel of Mercy! Prick! Lover! Mush! Run on
ya dog eared kiss willying nilly Dexter Michigan ass-war-
lerin ratpole! The rat in my cellar's an old canuck who
wasnt fooled by rebirth but b God gotta admit I was
born for the same reason I bring this glass to my lip — ?

Rut! Old God whore, the key to ecstasy is forever-
more furthermore blind! Potanyaka! God of Mercy!
Boron O Mon Boron! All of ye! Rush! Ghosts & evil spir-
its, if you appear I'm saved. How can you fool an old
man with a stove & wine drippin down his chin? The
flowers are my little sisters and I love them with a dear
heart. Ashcans turn to snow and milk when I look. I
know sinister alleys. I had a vision of Han Shan a dark-
ened by sun bum in odd rags standing short in the
gloom scarey to see. Poetry, all these vicious writers
and bores & Scriptural Apocraphylizers fucking their
own dear mothers because they want ears to sell —

And the axe haiku.

All the little fine angels amercyin and this weary
prose hand handling dumb pencils like in school long
ago the first redsun special. Henry Millers everywhere
Fridaying the world — Rexroths. Rexroths not a bad
egg. Creeley. Creeley. Real magination realizing rock
roll rip snortipatin oyster stew of Onatona Scotiat
Shores where six birds week the nest and part wasted
his twill till I.

Mush. Wish. Wish I could sing ya songs of a perty

4

nova spotia patonapeein pack wallower wop snot polly
— but caint — cause I'll get sick & die anyway & you
too, born to die, little flowers. Fiorella. Look around.
The burlap's buried in the wood on an angle, axe
haiku. La religion c'est d la marde! Pa! d la marde! J m
en dor. —

God's asleep dreaming, we've got to wake him up!
Then all of a sudden when we're asleep dreaming, he
comes and wakes us up — how gentle! How are you
Mrs Jones? Fine Mrs Smith! Tit within Tat — Eye within
Tooth — Bone within Light, like — Drop some little
beads of sweetness in that stew (O Phoney Poetry!) —
the heart of the onion — That stew's too good for me
to eat, you! —

People, shmeople

4   Boy, says Old Angel, this amazing nonsensical rave
of yours wherein I spose you'd think you'd in some
lighter time find hand be-almin ya for the likes of what
ya davote yaself to, pah — bum with a tail only means
one thing, — They know that in sauerkraut bars, god
the chew chew & the wall lips — And not only that but
all them in describable paradises — aye ah — Old
Angel m boy — Jack, the born with a tail bit is a deal
that you never dream'd to redeem — verify — try to
see as straight — you wont believe even in God but tbe
devil worries you — you & Mrs Tourian — great gaz-zuz
& I'd as lief be scoured with a leaf rust as hear this poe-
tizin horseshit everyhere I want to hear the sounds thru
the window you promised me when the Midnight bell

on 7th St did toll bing bong & Burroughs and Ginsberg were asleep & you lay on the couch in that timeless moment in the little red bulblight bus & saw drapes of eternity parting for your hand to begin & so's you could affect — & *ee*ffect — the total turningabout & deep revival of world robeflowing literature till it shd be something a man'd put his eyes on & continually read for the sake of reading & for the sake of the Tongue & not just these insipid stories writ in insipid aridities & paranoias bloomin & why yet the image — let's hear the Sound of the Universe, son, & no more part twaddle — And dont expect nothing from me, my middle name is Opprobrium, Old Angel Midnight Opprobrium, boy, O.A.M.O. —

Pirilee pirilee, tzwé tzwi tzwa, — tack tick — birds & firewood. The dream is already ended and we're already awake in the golden eternity.

5   Then when rat tooth come ravin and fradilaboodala back-ala backed up, trip tripped himself and fell falling on top of Old Smokey because *his pipe* was not right, had no molasses in it, tho it looked like a morasses brarrel, but then the cunts came. She had a long cunt that sitick out of her craw a mile long like Mexican Drawings showing hungry drinkers reaching Surrealistic Thirsts with lips like Aztec — Akron Lehman the Hart Crane Hero of Drunken Records came full in her cunt spoffing & overflowing white enlightened seminal savior juice out of his canal-hole into her hungry river bed and that made the old nannies gab and kiss that.

6

6   0 he was quite racy — real estate queen — Europe
& Niles — for pleasure — stom stomp absulute raze
making noise — I can write them but I cant puctuate
them — then he said comma comma comma — That
skinny guy with black hair — Atlean Rage — in India in
the last year he's getting even ignoring all common pub-
lications & getting Urdu Nothing Sanskrit by Sir Yak Yak
Yak forty page thing Norfolk — let's all get drunk I
wanta take pictures — dont miss with Mrs. lately in
trust picture pitcher pithy lisp — that's an artistic kit
for sex — Trying to think of a rule in Sankrit Mamma
Sanskrit Sounding obviously twins coming in here
Milltown Equinell Miopa Parte Watacha Peemana
Kowava you get sticky ring weekends & wash the tub,
Bub — I'll be gentle like a Iamb in the Bible —
Beautiful color yr lipstick thanx honey — Got a match
Max? — Taxi crabs & murdercycles — Let's go to
Trilling & ask him — I gotta wash my conduct — Dont
worry about nothin — I love Allen Ginsberg — Let that
be recorded in heaven's unchangeable heart — Either
bway — Rapples — Call up Allen Price Jones — Who is
that? — They re having fun on the bed there — Soo de
ya bee la — And there came the picture of Ang Bong de
Beela — Fuck it or get it in or wait something for the
bee slime — Then the ants'll crawl over bee land —
Ants in bands wailing neath my bloody ow pants, owler
pants — Ta da ba dee — He thinlis I'm competive in a
long pleasant souse of Wishing all of ye bleed stay medi-
tation everybody martini destroy my black — Allen ye
better voice the stare, this beer these room sandwiches

— Where did you get these? Big greasy socialists — Are you gonna konk, Allen? Mighty tall in the saddle — Anybody got a ceegiboo? — The moon is a piece of tea — (Under the empty blue sky, vertebrate zoology.)

7   And make the most malign detractor eat from the love of the lamb — and the pot that's for everybody not diminish when somebody comes — Tathagata, give me that —

Visions of Al

Women are so variously beautiful it's such a pleasure

Think happy thoughts of the Buddha who abides throughout detestable phenomena like lizards and man eating ogres, with perfect compassion and blight, caring not one way or the other the outcome of our term of time because celestial birds are singing in the golden heaven. In the golden hall of the Buddha, think, I am already ensconced on a tray of gold, invisible and radiant with singing, by the side of my beloved hand, which has done its work and exists no more to tone up the troubles of this birth-and-death imaginary world — And that's because the Old Angel Midnight is a Fike — that's because the Old Angel Midnight never was. And the story of love is a long sad tale ending in graves, many heads bend beneath the light, arguments are raving avid lipt and silly in silly secular rooms silly seconsular rooms full of height agee — Swam! reacht the other shore, folded, in magnificence, shouldered the wheel of iron light, and shuddered no more, and rowed the fieldstar across her bed of ashen samsara sorrow towards in here, the bliss evermore.

So.

Saw sight saver & fixt him. — Love you all, children, happy days and happy dreams and happy thoughts forevermore —

Dont forget to put a dime in the coin box by dipping your finger in ancid inkl the holy old forevermore holy water & bleep blap bloop the sign a the cross, when facing the altar down the aisle when you're waltzing — Ding! Up you go, smoke

8   The Mill Valley trees, the pines with green mint look and there's a tangled eucalyptus hulk stick fallen thru the late sunlight tangle of those needles, hanging from it like a live wire connecting it to the ground — just below, the notches where little Fred sought to fell sad pine — not bleeding much — just a lot of crystal sap the ants are mining in, motionless like cows on the grass & so they must be aphyds percolatin up a steam to store provender in their bottomless bellies that for all I know are bigger than bellies of the Universe beyond — The little tragic windy cottages on the high last cityward hill and today roosting in sun hot dream above the tree head of seas and meadowpatch whilst tee-kee-kee-pearl the birdies & mommans mark & ululate moodily in this valley of peaceful firewood in stacks that make you think of Oregon in the morning in 1928 when Back was home on the range lake and his hunting knife threw away and went to sit among the Ponderosa Pines to think about love his girl's bare bodice like a

fennel seed the navel in her milk bun — Shorty
McGonigle and Roger Nulty held up the Boston Bank
and murdered a girl in these old woods and next you
saw the steely green iron photograph in True Detective
showing black blotches in the black blotch running cul-
vert by the dirty roadside not Oregon at all, or Jim Back
so happy with his mouth a blade of grass depending —

Hummingbird hums
hello — bugs
Race and swoop

Two ants hurry
to catch up
With lonely Joe

The tree above
me is like
A woman's thigh
Smooth Eucalyptus bumps
and muscle swells

I would I were a weed
a week, would leave.
Why was the rat
mixed up
in the sun?

Because Buddhidharma came from the West with dark eyebrows, and China had a mountain wall, and mists get lost above the Yangtze Gorge and this is a mysterious yak the bird makes, yick, — wowf wow wot sings the dog blud blut blup below the Homestead Deer — red robins with saffron scarlet or orange rud breasts make a racket in the dry dead car crash tree Neal mentioned "He went off the road into a eucalyptus" and "it's all busting out," indicating the prune blossoms and Bodhidharma came from the India West to seek converts to his wall-gazing and ended up with Zen magic monks mopping each and one and all and other in mud koan puddles to prove the crystal void.

W o w

9   Lookin over der sports page I see assorted perms written in langosten field hand that wd make the 2 silhouetted movie champeens change their quiet dull dialog to something fog — ah, Old Angel Midnight, it will be all over in a year.

Dying is ecstasy.

I'm not a teacher, not a sage, not a Roshi, not a writer or master or even a giggling dharma bum I'm my mother's son & my mother is the universe —

What is this universe
    but a lot of waves
And a craving desire
    is a wave
Belonging to a wave

in a world of waves
So why put any down,
 wave?
Come on wave, WAVE!
The heehaw's dobbin
 spring hoho
Is a sad lonely yurk
 for your love
Wave lover.

I would I were a little tiny Jesus examining the mystery above the lightbody-cloud of the moon on still Marin nights, the flowers are my moon goddesses, & take craps naked. Horrible delightful the old retired harridan joys that wobble on the walking stick hill with nervous Collies yarking Yowk here in Journal Town where I wobble the card crate prayer bead Juju box with swing of wordage while Chas Olson reads my prose, man of the broad mysterious smoky Mountain Morn. (And everything is non-existent), heh. —

In a universe of waves quel difference betwixt one wave & t'other? T s all the same wavehood & every little unlocatable electron is a Tathagata pouring electromagnetic gravitational light at the constant speed of light (which can be heard in the sound of silence) & so this endless radiation of mysterious radiance is merely the minutia magnificent endless Tathagata Womb manifesting itself multiply & so not at all, for, all things are no-things but if this bores you it's because you want bricks in your soup. Empty.

The Happy One is free
It's a mystical mystery
It's endless light
The golden eternity

Why read Don Quixote when you can read The Diamond Sutra or the Wonderful Law Lotus Sutra? Why read Mickey Spillane when you can read Gary Snyder & Philip Whalen & the Mexico City Blues? Why hide what you mean behind natural data?

What does it mean that True Nature is incomprehensibly beyond the veil of our senses and is like empty light? It means that True Nature is incomprehensibly beyond the veil of our senses & is like empty light. If someone were to say to me, Krap, cart your daddy over here & let's hear tarbey? I'd say Wap, how'n you can cray that way when small fot find out all Sond your Oo like Where you like me & You Like Me & OO La Koo Me the onta logical philosizer fonted in the crap ding? He'd say, Froo, this Sunday Blues is too tree drunk & dead tree, & I'd say push out the cork & can it, vant more moonshine potatovodka or go to church or tet, shet, the Lord is all this.

The American Dreamer
Star of Karuna
The Moon of Pity
Ti Jean

A grat big sweaty wave — You get a vision of the truth as the universe of electrical waves all of it pure ecstasy then you open the old sutras and all you see no matter how many pages you turn over is human egoism

& warnings — bah — I am the new Buddha — and I shall call myself ELECTRON — Why the all this hassel over what you do when there's no time no space no mind just illusion & mystery? It's sheer ignorance & old-fashion'd God fear — Why shd I fear Myself? — It's like looking at a movie high & insteada the story you see swarming electrical particles each one a bliss fwamming in the screen eternally — shit! I'm going to the other side.

I dont need precepts

I need love

I need the Vision of Love

VISIONS OF LOVE

This holy and all universe is a wonderful white wild power, why, hell, should, heaven, interfere, words, waiting, flesh, sure, I, know, write, poems, this is no way to make it into the blessedness sweetly to be perceived, believed, & acted upon. Be silent & real. I feel very displeased, I just stood on my head & my neck is sore. But I'll jump like a gazelle at six. Good God how can I ever die standing on my head each day 5 minutes?

I feel very pleased now, 5 minutes later. The whole system is washed both ways. I'll invent a packboard that you haul up yourself, lashed, to a pulley, & tie to a bit, & hang upsidedown at ease, for old age. For this is the True Way. It is gravitational forces. It makes me eat & run into the yard & wash & forget all about electrical.

Dont touch me, I'm full
of snakes
(say the psychopathic flips)

Fanny fancy —
thou done
That crap

Gary (Snyder) gone
like smoke
— My lonely shoes
My rugged huge blue shoes

10   Morning sun —
the purple petals,
Four have fallen

Somavilerd, who thot that no one loved him, got
himself reborn a dozen million times in various-around
world systems in order to prove that the reason was
his own detestableness, but his detestableness didnt
belong to him because there is no ego owning going on
anywhere in the universal dream only endless talk &
twaddle & tales of idiots — told for nothing & waving
like leaves of a sea of trees in the birdy tweeking morn-
ing when motors & valleys bourk — Fanny the Spider
built a web from sill to flower stem, pot, winejug, &
Donlin declined — Iing ba twa laramenooki Wi the
bugs interwooped like zing planes in the heatening
mornlull & full sperm spof smudge re testified the

empty fertilities with a new mistake — milky mistakes abounding & spoffing everywhere from crap cellars to courtesan silkbed in Minarette — & all went to prove that in the golden eternity old angel midnight never happened & in North Beach the cold hopeless fog mist on Monday Morning, after binges with Sublette & Donlin who sleep all day & only wake to drink another jug — I dont understand this suffering but there's no ego owning in sufferunderstanding either — And all the combined sounds one hummin gnoise — Cats yawn I'd like to yawn I'd like to not like and begone bechune & bejesus if what on earth & under heck & over shit we gonna do O hopeless ghosts? — IL PICCOLO CAFFE what they do there, Vallejo! — I'd never've known f twasnt for Ma & Pa — As many times' I relight the Wizard Pipe it goes out — That's the store — nothing hidden the stash is a free treasure — God aint cached — All I take in I put out again, it's a filthy channel designed to drive me mad — Lo Lord what did I buy, what did you sell? What kinda bamboo poles you got in that merlasses brarrel of Yours, Avalokitesvara? — Shut up & let the nose go — try not asking — spiratual ecstasy is nothing — the rhinestone in the juju is the rhinestone in the juju, & your table she's small — and yr wife put you out & screwed a Porto Rican — the jumble of events is a thing — I'll ask why till I fly. The potter dwelling in his humble claypot strung this rote together to while the whelom along the dry clay woman bank where children cling to their mother's back & Father's Falling — into Mother — bing bang the Yabyum News — bing bang

16

the bolt in the void — Pop ping the electromagnetic in
the gravitational the yang in the yin — the positive mak-
ing the negative different, the negative holds the posi-
tive, & so I'm sick — & so I know — I'm sick — Sugata

11 Laurel Dell camp, boo! Cow swung my shirt
around, deers hooftrompled my sleep, moon was like a
streetlamp in my face, & I didnt sleep till the big cat
who came down the pyramid wall in the morning
where I told Ma about Mamie Eisenhour's drunk & I got
my diploma & we landed & she threw her ice cream
drunk & I was glad about something ephemeral & dur-
ing the night I willed to leap outa my sleep wildly but it
took some dead & inert time — the Book of Dreams &
all my words, hurt — I'm goin back to my cabin &
write Sweet Mother & Son slowly & gladly

12 Lou Little explaining to the newsreel audience
how this football player went mad & shows how on a
Columbia Practice Hillside it started with father & son,
the gray reaches of the Eternity Library beyond — I go
visit my sweet Alene in her subterranean pad near the
3rd Avenue El & Henry St of old Mike Mike milkcan
Ashcan Lower Eastside Dreams & pink murders & there
she wont ope the door because I cant get the job I tried
so hard to get & the woman said my form wasnt right
but Neal made it but regretfully it is he's shipping, out
& I'm on the ship with him telling him "If you wash
dishes dont say a word, if you're a yeoman do yr work
all well" — I can see he hates to go without me to this

other Grayshore — Sitting before my stove on a cold gray Saturday morning with my coffee & my pipe, eating jello — remembering the little jello cartoon that filled me with such joy as a kid on Sarah Avenue, the little prince wouldnt take pheasant or delicate birds or celestial puddings or even Mominuan Icecream but when the little bird brought him jello inverted in a rill mold cup he went wild & saved the kingdom, red jello like mine, in the little dear lovable pages — of long ago — My form is delight delight delight

Ring, ring, ring —
Shh, the sky is empty —
Shh, the earth is empty —
Look out, look in, shh —
The essence of jello is the essence of arrangement —

Be nice to the monster crab, it's only another arrangement of that which you are

13 Bobby Mathews of Philadelphia & Ed Crane of NY accomplished the feat before 1900 (striking out 4 men in 1 inning) — O those old ballgames, O lost Foleys of South Boston in old time Boston raw drump drunk days I love you — Geo Hooks Wiltse of the Giants did it on May 15, 1906 when my father was 17 years old in his pinksuspendered primal origin blues — when Old Jacques Kerouac raved behind the woodstove on church sunday mornings with his jug & today is May 28 1956 & me & Bob Donlin (Donnelly of Visions of Gerard) are drinking port in McCorkle's shack & the wind roars thru the shoh trees — Alright, mothers &

sons, I'll write for ye & tell a long sweet dad tale — For all is the same happy purity! Ya, padawaddy I like to frail them broadies Peer Engeli icecream backseat redleather creamcome fuck O cone! — let me love you again, sweet baby — this will do till nextyear's orgasm do — overhead levy assembling eastboat taxers hotson foundries bringin Alene Melville to my motherlovin arms Ah sweet indescribable verdurous parapineta post-wallowing rail ron hung on bu-bu-Angel's Telephoto let Anita Ekberg Pali shorts & all thu — so Miss'sippi Gene could go Hmf in his trance car blues — Why dash? — Sip.

14 Because while Gore Bedavalled marvels he steps, Ole Robeflow, from isle to isle into Mrs Roocco's windrow to innerstate the gas meek and bring photons, neutrons, pootons, borons, & oromariavalosa perstarolingish pert part pomerance poons, Topki, to flash in the mokswarm smugbug television vision intertaining trains twain by trallis — radamasanthus the watermelon bone — Higgins diddle, the redsox sunboys'll be in 4th place June & 5th place december & that's all, beancod — On top of Vulturesque Desolation the train orders'll oughta be simpler than twine 4 Engineer's an old anarchistic fud — Shoot, pot, proms were flowery purple lilac Richmond eve roadsters redlegs sweetdolls & wild palms bleeding on the reincarnated seabach father pramming oysters in a poppy corn basket with holy scowl — Robeflow disappears into the Golden Age with a falting tired didnt-make-it hand like Homer blind Demosthenes Dumb & Aristophanes may squat on the Peloponnesian Xertian defeat of our times for this is Prak, the Greek Jew, the Canuck Hindu, prolling, purned, spoot, spout, teapot, drank, drilled, dripped, dvished, pish, tish. It was just a lottawords foir nathing — noneless the railyards produced littlegirls, & up above the boyshadows the stars as Karuna as ever burned mighty rot glows that evaginated & opened holy rose hopes Oh ho for the penisenvious thunderbers & boomdockers from Hook to Hey Here & heave that caffeine down, old ladycakes & frogmurder rivers & Angelo Noon running write a bleak glare inseparably terrified the parkinglots of destiny — it's all a lotta sand pilin up helplessly, harmlessly on itself obliterating the What Cave? If not oughta.

15   Let's dance — I go to your shack or you come to mine. Make a date. Do.
>   "Spring rain;
>>   it begins to grow dark;
>   Today also is over."
>>>   Care-a-Wack
>>>   Thus the dove advises —
>>>   I am woken to you —

16   Rabeloid! I cant breathe any more Mrs Jameson so will you please whore out? — I'm drinkin with the butchers, shut up! — if that doesnt sound kind it's because shittly aimed right at Tard & miss't with an 8-point aim that might do little over Tokyo but Kyoto throwed it — as the later testify will show these brunettes of peanut butter & hate were made were made were built & wellmade O crying children hurt! — So, I say, but knowing there's no me, Grub.

That's the saint

Stump — all on a stump the stump — accord yourself with a sweet declining woman one night — I mean by declining that she lays back & declines to say no — accuerdo ud. con una merveillosa — accorde tué, Ti Pousse, avec une belle femme folle pi vas' t' coucher — if ya dont understand s t t and tish, that langue, it's because the langue just bubbles & in the babbling void O Lowsy Me I'se tihed — If I'da who what? the perfect lil cloudy coroid cloud colorods colombing in the back fish tail twill twat of heaven blue — What's the blue, fly, what the drunk, fall, the wild upbuilding reinsurgence & Golden Ultimate Effulgence you'll find in Train No. Let's Go — to heaven — Bob Kauffman wants to come too — all aboard — You'll find that this train has six thousand compartments — Ring! — Hello — Rail, please — They're calling the Who Clerk — he'll give us the right rail we'll go to heaven sure — the sweet golden clime when the trav'ler's journey is done, under the hill, in a cool tomb — death was too proud so I stopt — we communed underneath nature — and so on — first level yr own mind then the earth is be level & no more mountains of hope — but just the slavic level flat expected crandall be-all & wise-all rhodomopordsomopholorophoshion crint

17 Saradalia wrote around the wrong rightness because he'd seen purple & gold visions swimming in consciously from the conscious ultra violet cosmic rays a the sun & fwang, twarl, tweeelll, twom, twerm I meant, Pearl, Immemorial Antequité Poil of Brooklyn Night-Bridge gray hope dreams sucking on the stairs the dead girl the new blues news of from Heaven endless radiations of magic blue salvation — Now how'd Kemp tell a fleapis when St. he'd a know'd there waint no Okie Song yander but Big Gorldpupple ringarond romp rillwash radamansus frallieng prodapiak, ratamita samantabhadra unceasing compassionate hope that with congruent bent stick as soon as he saw real deep & realized the lights were still there he understood he was a messenger, the Angel, one eye out — For Lucifer Moidner rant rag, rack, it's okay, these purloined potato perfunctory alliterative rubouts add up to sweet Popish Purple Paradise

18 San Francisco has no vaults — San Francisco has no vauty — Singalrad the sailor Sam said he saw in the so — Go — The students outside the monastery window have subsided in their chatter, light — Ran and farted to show his old rock routine & so "wom?" (Rom Tom?) (Vaii) hmf the noises (cloat) out the window, scratch, I Old Angel Midnight hear — Silent Indurm Twandee Yokle Hour when we'll begarret Sam Ashton Tom Belligerent the Hackett Master Beckett — Or sometimes lightly known as Yarp Yarp — Cop ski kimona moodia, Ah Su, tchétché, the cop coughs, I hear the taxio fi fu — old Monster Hufu the Zen Froofroo is now going to vain his glory by be shitting himself in gruel birth — Ning — Anais Nais Thaïs Ming — China Tink Hongya Ming Mon the Bong — Sing, & yack dank bar poets wont Listen to old Kanuck?

        Sarry, Said Sarie
     I'll Metemple You Mowley
        in the morning
         Betemple and me demple
   hey me that
         Tzimou m'appelle dans
         cour d'archelle
    Archangel Once Wing Swing
        Ah Sigh God
      Tu mar a ma danna
   tu dona, padrone
 Poura tu jama faire dire
    Tes grand
        ecritures?
Ecrivida
    Old Angel Midnigh rant rock
  rail rowout mo tarn
     rong igo I kfuck
     me j akle
       be dakle
    Mc Graw

19 Stop playing you candassed tripe heart, — common, let's have that aw story — lost your moidening rag

in the angry shack, & wick warnt long enuf you poota
— Sing for the general store of rain that will hail
bedown the —

20   "Spit on Bosatsu!" says Gregory Corso — "Oo
that's beautiful?" I say — Dash dash dash dash mash
crash wash wash mosh posh tosh tish rish rich sigh my
tie thigh pie in the sky — Poo on you too, proo the
blue blue, OO U Nu, hello Buddha man

21   Me — who was Old Angel Midnight that railed at
the rant & eat steak at the Met & threw ballet girls out
the hall & pinked with my wife in a shower bath —
Beautiful blue Jean Marais, the denzing champion
of Europe — rurt — Bing bing — the flames of the can-
dle say 'Leave us alone, we have a lil ole window of
our own & we happen to know too that the whole
Universe is saying' — 'Shut up you moidnees and mar-
deners and gardens of marden, man, silt soft silt the
sound we ray — We weigh everything in the scale of
time, I say, pajestically plurting in the perfect platoon
— illiterate me that — but tramwise, tranways, what'd
you mean, tranways, tramways? — Oi, Russia has funny
scrolly drawings broodled on midnight doodle pad,
we'll never see — But Shostakovich know me, & candle
fall — Burt — Was Burt was the sweet star swang in the
hall and was killed in the war and nobody I know of
cried — Old Angel rant shack mack Mill Valley rack
shap, map, dap tag was bon tailored when I win-gee
was Prez —

No, Prez never presented no such horn like that, Prez was the bezz in the bizzness, man, mon, Prez was the end and the man on the end Prez was the champeen pole catcher in the world — the outstanding window the sound that came through

dwerrrrr

22 Old Angel Midpike, wasnt the hike that was wedded to the fike? — the eyniard one-eyed piratical rat who ran roting thru the puderdical halls of Pwince bone yelling 'Hay to de tree Hay to de tree' and keppersnews the Viennese pastrymakin inkdweller pulled a party of sansi fancy sans souci dans and whammed em their spats, till Tillie the Late Tat, leaking from her holepot, organized redgangs to remnant his sin, and Jin, the magic bottle boy stolen from the Bagdhad ship shrouds routed Golgotha with a sling and arrow and had all the Queen Mother Superiors gasping in parks — Remember it quite well and well aint he coming home late? Twang in the window and see if he'll tweak his old beard at ikonoclastical me, poor dear — Dolophine robin roved a long way to bring balm to soothe his blue bus — Well like I was sayin, and anyway atchoo, your water's boilin, aint you? — Not much I can do about it Mrs Twandow as seeing as my Sandusky Husband comes home driving in the green light tho he's colorblind, he traded all the sneakthieves & secret narcotic police to the Virgin on the Wall, & she et em up raw like candle wax — His old father upfaced in a tomb — His knives and forks on top his cakes — His "hands burning" — a la Gregory Corso — His use of Gleem toothpaste in canvases — No joke, son, that wall has more ears than Ebon'll allow — How many ears that wall? — as many ears as you got lights in all space everywhere every atom's on fire — hands — How gruesome the smoketacle of people burning in rooms — the yurn of their faces when the airoplane crashes — Ah Mrs Midnight I cant understand — You understood this afternoon when you hung out the wash — Yes I hook out the wash with a crook of my thumb, & whistled so sharp and hubby came home and kissed me too — but now's playing cribbage at Vicious McStoo — Oi oi pearl, pearl of the sea, flow through my window, bring whiteness and money and honey to me, bring hunner to me, bring butter and knives and archives and archangels bring them all to me and Molly Magee of Dublin Bloom — bring that to me, wall-ears — Sky's only got a fartin passage for you babe, message, what you expect from bean chamberpots and laundry in the lavenderia washingmachine, you expect roses? or worms? oi? You expect howling storms? — smath me to smithereens this aint the Bronx — if itn was the Bronnex I'd cancel it — cank — konk all you want on your juicy window, mirror-face, I'se a old lady was weaned i the bowels of the air the earth what's the big difference between air & between earth? — Ai, pickles in the barrell, and poetry too, but what's with your husband aint comin home early like he used to bechunes? — S Writ in the cards of my mother's birthveil — Ojaya Ojaya the company buzzes throughout the world in a hundred thousand cities of rooms, the ha dal baddra of their midnight babble, all talkin at the same time, NOW, — Oi poor humans beings, I grieve for you — I been in steel jails but Oi, it was no worse than the best that was it of the this — When I sent cans of Accent to Greece disguised as heroina I didnt have poolhalls in my basin — I had basinettes made of lapels and bassettes (brass badinettes for strange badinage —)

23 Spat — he mat and tried & trickered on the step and oostepped and peppered it a bit with long mouth sizzle reaching for the thirsts of Azmec Parterial alk-lips to mox & bramajambi babac up the Moon Citlapol — settle la tettle la pottle, la lune — Some kind of — Bong! — the church of St. All's blasts the Ide afternoon & all holy worshippers go confess to Father Everybody with Good Friday ears — Friday afternoon in the universe —

Bong! — the twackle how wackle of high Berkeley parties, the twanging and walking and cops carrying guns, *bong!* the church bell of Ah Ide the Master Hunchback primavera Cat of the Soiled Star universe — and him with his Priam — Well I never, and late at that, and's got cramps

Bong! the midnight the mirror the red rust of the rosy atmosphere of the ikon the candle the babyface sleeping —

Bong! enough of the bell dear Lord God above, enough of the eeny miney mo bell

Bong! — alright Mr. Poe, Mrs. Twurn, Mr. Twart, rart, I'd like to indicate by moon medallion indicative half-ass magic your prophesy, & what fool will post

make Lear of you, or what Twang-Bang arrow drape in
your vein, or Sicilian Stiletto in the streets of Old Spain
— Bong! if it's n midnight by now, mid nigh, by now,
I orta see myorta about a you know what er — horse
— er — man about a farting horse — man about a
Brooklyn Bridge — in brief excuse me I go shit — ugh!
Ow! — dont pull at my oliver twist ear!

24   The things they say that come in thru that window
— if only I could avoid what I hear —

Wasnt it Dostopoffsy who gossipped so much, and
that Balzac in *Cousine Bette* O my — And Tristram
Shraundy Shern, marvelous book, and Elmer Payo
Robinson, the author of Oogoon, and Shmarl
Baudelaire, the Skid rick rant rentfence iron night hold-
er (of Paris) over rooftops of smoking shame — Ole
Hornshaw too the Gerst poetizer, with Ilium and Troy,
and Inali Minoan Retreat the Great God Ur, that was
mailed to Philip Whalen — the samadhis of Hanse
Majesty, trop trick driver of mountains, Mt Baker and
Mt Olympus, parthenonical backtracker over old trails,
Schneider by name — Gossipers there're none like
Allan O Shinzberg, Levinsky my Feetsky, tweedy old
Mayo Opo Waldo Meldo Elmo Poe, the junkey from
Wall Street, and the Hawthorn person haw and sleet
Melville who made subterraneans live in rooftops of
shame in the shadow of the Brooklyn Bridge and John
Holmes creamed (the aunorthist not the noet) — Hang
my fryinpan cover over a nail, wont you, & I'll bank the
ikon — and turn on electric light, and see what I'm eat-

ing here, hairs of 19 0 ten —

Poo! prat! two taxis played two little musics — then "brrrrrrrrrinsss" big gugly whatname truck came by signifying the nothing of the sound afternoon —

25 Like's legs that goosed the underground schoolteachers & Joyce who always wanted to write blind what the sea said but grinned restoredly in the sea first, himself a gable of coral roan, hears now in my behalf the scree of old railroad iron twisting faggot cargos of ESYirt by the shiney MOsoon vessels of the Packet Bay to bring elum slippery to Gaza & the Strip of Fez where donziggerls grab boycocks — easy as pie that window Islam sea roar, that purebeacon, that Sherifian splendour, that Lustre Magno hide in the Me high hill Virgin Ma Wink — so's on opium old Joe Black come home hammock Florida tree-hack — I heerd that HEAL pass thu — I feeled it pass that heal by thu — I seed that hole the hail made — And if in every window hovel would words sung beard prophet flip nothing mean, then hie thee New Gab Haven bring lice shit rooms to steel necktie lover of tomb, never heard a nanny bray like that — Old Angel Midnight Worldwindow bong midnight interlude Eternal Already

26 Old Angel Midnight just writes itself as it is the Hi-Is Sound — miracles of Jesus in Capernaum — so that it might be all fulfilled as twas writ in Akashia — but see the future writ in present state illumina — what does the horizon of the sea got to do with singing boy? —

John Kerouac transliterator of perfect knowing, angel from heaven, messenger of the right hand of God & of the Godness of All hath no warm place to lay his head but must cover his knees with both hands & despair, the great weight of bleary time —

27 Ah but Old Angel Midnight Africanus the message in the dream block roundsquare tenement boom from the submarine Joandream ships, destroyers & escorts, putput fez & all rhythm fishermen sprayling in the bay sand — Trumpets blare by the moon sea the Arabs barge to redhat olivegreen majesty & old black scow ESPERAN-TO — movies about that. Vast stupid Kerouac-o ——

28 Light the candle to the continuation of the hot afternoon Ah now I see she's turning gold & working-men are done till Monday Morn & come home on now straight with buckets to their dens, lions all balls — dash, Bach Chevrolet — Even the 2 lil Chinese hog-moyens are propping along beneath the Tall Silk Void anxious to get in ere tree twisted to rock plum blos-soms — Plump haired belt dog pop O looksee where the redheaded spreaded her leglets at last in the Midden, & in Spain the Capernaum call of children Chorus boys "There's nothing like our religion" so sew the dress & wait for the golden electricity to make you right — for you know, Big Oldie, your maw's right & she waits for you midden plumps to ard out more poly-chromatic Spirochete to mix like Marble fudge in that Tchelitchev Tree of Life & bring forth busting another prime plump poy for your posy grave & they'll say wasnt that my Ard Craven Bard Bar Pap I saw upfaced to Tomb? — No, that was the Eternal Consoler passing thru as Knife yard, his white shirt knit by Rimbaud Angels did sweep aside the river mud from this intact and classify crystal, so that so-that could soolidat smarty pine — Ah, yar — but she yawed so much & I had to be saved from drunken bumhood by these words, will excuse me if cant read my jazz right because this floorboard language'll hide bettern nails the Emily Dickinson worse-than-ever dahlic drent bent despair of me with my raw muscles bulging in the mirror of pride, lank low face all set to prove novels as soon's crick goes soring out the other side my arm I'll tell you een more but now it's comin on Friday night & GLEE yell the children of Paris running over the grass of St. Thomas d'Aquin where supplicatee hold artistic Europe oil hand out to be larded poignarded bathed powdered put away ah all the Napoleonic troubles in this pastry! — Tie it all together, Jack, the mirror doesnt show the real right

29 Eternally I accuse you of being as craven a shit as Frank ever planked on that Leo butcher board so's mice could be crying safe in the arms of Jesus — the Little Christ! You! Why dont you mind your bexness! The less I hear of em the happier I'll be! Do I have to come back in another lifetime or next month & let you have it where you need it so's I can live my private label life free of libellous old you, continuous old Cronk tokay ass hole hurrying to your place to be maitled & draigled

& dragged & even hipe Wop Cork knows you you scandalmonjous gossipping non Dostoevskyan shit of the ages! I'll flow golds of venom thru your window & you receive it all like some old Universe SLUT — What kinda man are ya, Slut? Or what kind good slut can you be anyhow with no twat to tie it? You & your marble wax samsarhood burning up nothing but candles of worry hate & shame, bug wart pastyfaced *bustard!* — I'll cut your head off with my machete fingernail, & yak make crack your Orienral thats what you want faces, I'll fix you, Gossip! Old Flap of the Shrouds, sheet on the line, Twandow shit, shirker, fuckface of history, go home & blow yr wife & leave mine & mine alone! — O o o o r g ! G o o o r d ! B l o o o d ! — I'll have your pasty flesh feed for Merrimac fish another time corpse you Joan kid crack bedeviller fool & Faust fuck! Who wants your dirty Old Words? — Pray for us on Hester street, dear Lord, do you exist? Pray, for us on Arameia Street, dear sweet save-me Lord — Save me Lord is just it, *you*, alone, let the others boil in marsh harrico, slong as you can slomp & fall in your slop barrell — no *words* boy to describe it — What? — Your *hate* fulness! Your hatful of emptyheaded raindrops! I orter throw you off the fire escape, myorter, wouldnt do no good, you with your headstands come back the next day all healed (hear me boy, just kiddin) — you're a good enuf old boy but my God you write too much.

But I'm only reporting the sounds out the window?

Well gate a fet reporter & go call charlie in the bar, turd, and find your old Peace & pink in yr own home showers & leave Fitzgerald alone & Marcus Magee or go strangle bobbies in the fog, do something butt dear God in the Arse, leave me alone & MINE!

Ah Angel Midnightmare —

Ah Crack Jabberwack, play piano, paint, pop your pile anum coitus semenized olium o hell what's his biblical name, the pot that spilt in the room ere Sarad had hers, ad her share, the name, the word, for masturbators, the Neptune O YA you know the name, the Bible Keen Mexican yowl that old tree still hangs in the same moonlight — Ilium, Anum, Ard Bar, Arnum, Odium, Odious, *ONAN!* ONAN KERAQUACK go heal yr own toiletbowl, stop dropping shavings in mine, & leave my grave unsung, my death unlearn, my qualities you can have, but onanist no quarter given you Angel Midnight by in that holy gallows of the moon!

Do I dream?

You dream not, switch yr dolophine midnight bell bong on some other frequency — *dont you know?*

Know what?

That there's a white cross marked X in the road where you will die yr dog's death & there to burn the piffle on your pier the ship will take you straight to golden essence & you be still?

Meanwhile?

While mean you mean well? Switch houses, try Killiams!

Junior Killiams, that laird Cregar'd high big muff moitang mouk moity biff jaw?

Same, with sluggerous pall in the ach —

In the ach & ah part tooth ache of peotly? The prime love thighs not for me but bearded shit not listen see till tee give me ernest majesgetafree? Why?

Because foiled the poor luke bird.

Fuke the luke fool bird foiled, I want oil!

Take oil in other Shelves.

Message received.

Close your window.

I'll open it tonight.

Let the stars fart their message unpolluted by human one, please hee?

You that bonged dolefully with benign crasher on yr head in old heroic dawns —

Ach, same, shamed, let me nightsoil be —

United purefoy Clown.

Besides you kill bugs with the rash of your pencil deed crashing on holy ivory love papers meant for scented notes from sweet jissom creatures clacking down the Barnard trees — Wash your drawers, draw the river in, pull that grave dung reward over yr noble nose, blow out the Candle & if you fail is that hardest on me?

I'll go mad as a bush.

And burn, please, the hardwood floors hiding me.

30 Mindscreaming blood perturbation pisspot — Mindscreaming blackjack Lanka Mountain laughter —

You're making it all up so why worry about being or not being? Thus rolls The Angel Midmoke

31   Put put put tiPousse all's to go well your mew gold taken good care of you, no only roan neigh yak plan reign can slay that rose oboed flow soul I robed you say satin devil — Jesus will bring you all — Wait'll the music starts, little flicks of millionfold billionminded fleet stars thronging all for a chance to live try sentience come swamming down your hard vale, whyfor hardvale boy? — Did I seek to bore your butter heart with mod iron skew in ogly scag iron bottomed ogroid doididoidee worlds bestrew your natural sweetness avant? No because loved you, love you now, no words of Mortal disfamous postifillication & bile pow gonna ruin my blue eyed pootuin toot where happily sanging frank lark lovely bardo. — No. — So let heaven instruct thee, earth no bug thee, go fly as free as you wish to be, sing window bedelong bidiliyoukidiligoo sweetsweet Tu Fu bird oriol paradise Chinee garden all ya want! — Soft, you my dangle gentle playful little pip leak I bring you deliverance but you must listen to Daddy Snow arms when's he got to say to you: — pat on the folld

32   Brrrrring back the early wave, pearl — now cometh upon us the time when diamonds shatter, all love & hope gone, all tirlish bang, all fort might be dizened underneath the snow white salt wall, all lost undersea blue lips buried in grime of guilt in this crystal clarity recall, all bugs burned in the Raid of Time and all fard heard none such scone throw yield nothing but goom & booboos — poof! — The child, the circle

drawn in air, the primal matter primal substantial ener-
gy polled & lost two votes elect the last twat & tit you
too, I hope the diamond shatters into a billion glittering
smithysheens of Croo because now Lustrous Midsoil I
been pointed out, begallowed, hung, prophesied,
Karma'd, Kaught & kitkatted up the ass of God Guilt &
when I turn my back on this poor world I got no back
to do it with, who will forgive the scribbling devil?
When Snow Dad armed me with promises not kept &
blamed me & booted me seedy cold hills, urk, ouch, my
hand hurt, I tell you I wont tell you no more, why
should I poignard me old shoulderblade with this
machete matter? And country matters decide cities
full of hurt children buried in the groomus womb of
Bellevue Morgue — And fly stars purporting and all p's
& pop it, blaming poor children for sighing under trees
while long white trail ghosts swish in the river's foam-
ing mouth, like semen at the crock rotch math both
Falls of Indio Doom, say, hark, promising star of home-
father did you not pull sod blanket over baby's eyes &
when you'd by his crib painted pink happy images of
angels disporting ogre ord holes that turned to door
opening monsters — monstranot love, mama dears — I
was opiumed & killed in ole Tangiers — Every hate
filled Arab & American in the world shall write explana-
tion on a bier, every priest draw his bread clanging
pisspots of grime, every philosopher suck up the
claimant genius for his lifehood gold, every critic shit,
every fancy poet fall, every bear devour Elijah rex
rot, & every publisher & scribe be Pharisee'd in

Castiglione's gloomy rager — me? my name? and I? go off father son & holy ghost of Martyr Life — And I will be silent, answer you no dong, Going Smock Syrup Midfuk, shit pearl pot, whatzyername, Luke Degger, erp urp rain watt Arkansaw south foil follow-up crooks & trees, I've had my roody filler that nard sauce & I'm going to die now, breath no more words pain on this silver & worry hatepage, I am the moth I killed in infant desire Hemming & Waying page of teen — London Jacked & Lusted the Liver out of me, been raped by sister king & knifed by brother queen & now all's I gotta do is appreciate the hardness & emptiness of rocks & go curfew & an old man in his hunchy death, sleek — purtier than Ava Gavovnar, more eepish than sic fop hat gargoyle Boilio the poet of the Lower West Side mural, gangster popoff racketeer evil slander murder shit kill quit cut fuck rape scream howl pump kill gate murder down imp I'se re gusted — because there never was a better opening than because —

Hear my song free stars, yet I can reach swelling moist, cunt of heaven admit my rod of justice, halls of Old Nirvana here comes Diamondshatter shat diamonds gave birth to Tathagata Garbha got blamed for Tranadaz & kilt in McQuentin & Mill Vallied st john hill gold huan so's *huan* one world could creep satisfaction to the creeps of literature

33   Foo, you yold yang

34 Then with balls swoled up one hung low leaving the action snake no biggern at, Oi, the lone woe of Lee Lucky his basketa pittykats earthquaking peoples balls outa sight & leaving nothing but tremble-under-the-bed, the grace in Orlando turned out to be a gentle wee heatwave & a little shit (O shut up and say it!)

35 Sor god denoder pie your pinging lief bring Ida Graymeadow Wolf babe ooo brooding in the is-ness seastand grayog magog bedonigle bedart ooo the day Odin meeteth the Loup Gris, yag, ack, the day ooo dies — The day the gray wolf oatses Odin for his long slack-jaw slaver, asurp — When Ida Meadows her long gown camp the Persian disencamps & dusts — When the vision fades from the rough surfaces of Snorri & Sturla — When Eric Bloodaxe and Harold Fairhair battle for the final blonde on the last Icelandic prick rock — When Rodedodo grows Chrysanthemums by the door — When Eugene Bonedown burps — When Hair Redknife snaps the band — When Callicott Cobcorny crashes in motherlip — When Orristander boos — When Whitlip barks — The dog days of Egypt, bow wow wow — When Espinal gives the bull his final ass — When visions of the sea go 152 — When Prick Neon's nailed to me! When Carrie Methodical Divine and the nomad Patzinak steppe bedazzlers (azzle dazzle muffed my gazzle!) the Napoleon fire rings, the slavers of the lip of Richelieu, Mazarin, Colbert, Lisieux, Ourmantelle, Archanciel and Pas D'Enfant kisses my ugly roar go-down seafeet on Oregon Beachie, when trappist divine speaking whistling the window roar borovates to the endless machine hum of endless infinitesimal worldspace oogloomosanical tarpidalisaclna multivantarn go-l-ta pian par music! — grag-ashash! — when burt me-davey-grave hung mine down poles the final lot across the rivie of Buddhas and last Potilic losts flint in the Old Star, ah me Marva, a flesh carney, ah river a day, ah strikeout, that's when I'll bring my lesson to thee, saith window to Me — And I cried "Window, what you mean?" Said window "O listen to the spherical booding moan star music the midnight study the Faust man devil harp in hand, O hum O moan O"

36   The little tit tat tadpole honey tweak of kitty lips on my toosy two toes make me think of dwiddle tingle springs the ditties of childerhood — sang — commanded Eyrdeadan showaps to crail before my fire ping! OOlamona! call the sails, the frog croak eave drip never-rains-but-sweats Florida screenwindow with Avaloki tes var star twarping in my woondow — And did you ever say the wee that nack saw all farding blle on par ton take sick grick clap cat mat cack Mother? No that was a halting burgle — purr — eat & purr be holy kittypee pool in sand of red eyed bat bird insewecties pirking tig toont ta Ma tire free curé the school — A long unlearned heavy school noises of piano legs in the smile paradise bed? I saw lines drop like lint off kittyfur nightbed brain thought & never heaved to Atlas Shrug Toad help flashlight God but instead as written in old behooven Diamond, say, "I am grown so old & neutral I

dont care" — Dont burn the cat! Second shelf for twickle cricket quiet cat held by nails go up fine smoke Burroughs in Tangiers'll smile smile smile — Thass iss the suundt com tatl patac mo jambi va shan tu vi maranoomavala ta ya ta ta the high ladder speech King Hank made glorp by Harfleur diners Stein bock bash Autumnal Beer Wolfe final window broken smash & cats say   Krut

37 Murzner, the murzning zamming ience ouch feections possessing this itch it-globe with everybody fawlderolling around a rat satellite, paff! — spat! — kipf! — I'd rather roll kief in Ten Restaurants with bandaged athletes of Arab Sand than fwaddle fwo with Ojo Ji JoJo the Immortal Shine afternoon kidder of the India Lawn wrestlingmatch with Fatty Arduffy the goateed Bull gainin on death by inches of pot lard & him with childrees in a crib! Oi! Ugh! Oirk!

38 Tonight in Russia command the rooftops to cry up Gogol Dos-*toy*-evsky & Ark to lief the irk-bear buried in Freeze Sand Siberia general electrified eet-freeze come out with hank of Scythian hair in his paw, stop burlying bloody bed back and under*stand*! Stand under sails of Callèd Ships, command whitemuff Alexander Long Island come out kill lieutenants at his baby's funeral & if Achilles rotted in a Paird Tent so did Mercedez when he bested Oilope the Troller of Spain rag, Zorro — when Inquisitional keeners of green fields Medieval Aromoratic Armorica Eraldic Rivistica Spoign bedang the sand of rucksack tearboys dying by my mother's thigh of gold — O dream! O Gary Snyder hero of compassion & poign! O Doll Marshall beautiful! My mind rings with a thousand iced lizard windows! I have no words for neutral! O poor bone burroughs in your yard in Tangiers, what cats seek ye to study now? The splendorossi ficuuiyus im-ling-star bangs around the landlady's angrified lawn & still the priests whirl mind rooftop pederast poignarx! —

Command Ardemuffin fire eaters cornmuffining in splott Lee Anne Burns the girlsinger from Hill Rich who when she throws her legs back has thighs of gold snap! Wtttasher name, Lu Anne Sins! Wow! Wait! Another forest primeval angel meet Hermyorter de Gingold play with Rheingold Princeton dark Lou Grossa punt ankle cock black as hairy murder in a lump of balls! Tie onta that, Pat! I aint got no more callings at crossings enemy diesel freeze, am gone to Rocky Mount flyin up to sunny cold flagwhip Philadelphia! So sing the song of All-Vard! Raise the hems of gold! Let sleep the peaceful ancient unclouded look of Sunday afternoon antcities in my merde murdered mind of moin — these parturiating pe-caco-ma-cunabulations in a Fireplace Suicide Attempt do bespeak a deeper purse than purpose John Roi who was overflowing with "poor perdu!

thin helm!"
the vision of
Medieval Europe
in a Shakespeare inch!

Hairbrush! Det! Wrench! Tont! Hanging sleepcloset stasified pearl cat color of dark retreat & maybe sink in back, I want the diamond shatterer bring it down return us dear Lord to Golden Aeternitatis.

39 Uncovered by the uncut version cheapmovie produced SWStarkike in High Heaven Lion roar Windtunnel never made the bestseller list of Nigeria but sold Jesus' last sad word to eager buyers & no Jesus to scat them out the temple — separate from every science fiction deaddog, go own neutral way, say nothing to airplanes on highways or obsolete stratagems of dinosaur battleships & all ye such crap & tiresome world fawdle, I'm telling you God I sure is glad you Is — I sure is glad you got star me Quixote bed cat & Ma love babies i' the house & Greyhound posts for buses — I sure is glad I wont have to perturb & gnaw on vulture lice erpastagraficus mona, name? Tergiratirus Pastrofian — crewa, crow — The silent dharma arhat crow of Florida coolnight makes my cats perk ears — So all ye merry gentle

40   men may say the word
    the high on t high
    earliest berv

41   the who dont care
    I dont care
    fuck you all
    word free
    Zen Lunacy

42   Rapt wrote ditties, Ruckus did: as Wit: in my mind
Bill is a feeling movie providing — pro*vid*ing? — snow
— *snow?* — for mosquito.

Mosquito of integrity not another State Funds suck
you integrity irregularity try Ex Lax perhaps ask ridicu-
lous state park fool or contract curtains exciting mos-
quitos fool by fool good day Brown Field — refuse!
These are the sounds of electricity pouring out of the
soldiers pension checks cheaper than fifty sentient vet-
erans who mailed their checks to Mr. Seriouscharge —
Ho! Window! Listen Gregory, science statement is mil-
lion years over owned by pens as treacherous as Aga
Arnold of Good Day Biddy Father Uptown — see? I'm a
fool! I love reverse! I got hidden Moo-Flutes in my horn
cow. I did it dad because I dood it money — I am
Governor President! Bled this state for years, Altruistic
politician cheat-anyone William did, & outsiders of
nothing lit trusted stolen money rotten dirty fires in
alumni bowery to celebrate the Five Percent dream!

Oig!

Forget!

The Burden Pen company was quilled a'ter the
name of Honest Tarnish Shakey Speary aspirer of cham-
pionship virtue & threatening son Hamnet, O Dad! My
conscience is all snow. In fact my conscience is
coldspot. Deny no crime, avow furiously, determined
accompanied company jury friends for Colonel Shoot

Hog to say "Sho was a niggerlover wasnt he?" So
Caroline with her wee wet spot out west wanted Bill
stick his Pelican in her key twat so she could yell
                    "Burt & Pen!
                        Burt & Pen!"
And that was how Innocent was born hating the
sight of me — ARtavasamagri! Famme twé! Battling the
nail, loose, my brain-pan doubled and I died crying I am
dead! When a boat parts water, dont look at people's
asses? Fill your glass with regal feeling beer cheer hap-
pening sun just naturally! Oranges are balls of sunshine!
Shut up!

43   That Christianity you have where the big fish does-
nt eat the little fish, is that the Christianity of the Cross?
        Yes, and of the Bo Tree, Cannibal

44   Birdleldeedlies in our morning fresh window, O
my darling sweetheart I miss you, a dum, a duma,
organs & light shake twickles and erdio poralondo
ogradar da the best fart test by far every swung that did
it so remember what God said to St Benedict in the
door of his cave at 6 AM in 892 "Live modern with
tile floors and walls" — And Danny & the Juniors
answered: "White Howl" — And Gregory the Great
wept big tears for the fall of Rome & the desecration of
Apostle Peter's Holy Seat

45   Honeymoon couples play phallic worship, be-
cause while the bride shows her breasts in a low

negligee the groom conceals hisun under pajama & bathrobes — Right? — "Let's go get some sleep darling" means "Be long" — Everybody that ever importuned boys in Portugal, or married glamorous young blondes in wartime knows this — Everybody knows the rod of justice — Eastern delinquent boat owners despair of airplanes — Niagara Falls Violins the tower of city canadian police — Look what silver girl is doing for gray hair! Arthur Paper Mate Flow Gem Buddha adorned by hair centuries of Buddhi Toni — Lotta talent in the Manger Bethlehem. The weather is Pew.

46 My soul's in my boots & my jockstrap holds up the stars hooray — Basie in London, O ye dreary backfences cheated me outa Limey Love on Waterlow Bridge and ann had a way, ya dreadful stargazing heaven of roof clup miz munk end-night fryingpan blaze gold silver material, all naught smashed & made unknown by blessed no-need catholic heaven saint Avalokitesvara, O — Now whisper, filter — Caint — You aint been to North Carolina Holyland of late — Sing, heaven brought honey dovey hero stars, spermfaced, open, grant, gone, gay, sweetliest must-arc auk mock honeybird of all friggling time — O my baby eateth pone pie, stands arms kimbing porch no-clothes cunthungry baby corn! — O child in Erse Love Bigstar Holyhood hunk crib! — O my mother! O secret Friendship!

47 Forty Which? O erse friendship, mak a laking smack tongue outa Luscious Midday moik out talk, hey then I'll pay you a hunnerd earnest children for your foy yoy candle coy-doy mingol bingle billshit pap outa me hang dont-let-em fuckoff flinging loc stare love time tak plot moy down Tangiers dreamy dreamies — See? Or bring curd yak lock lips lank hair legtledptay monshine — See? or drink less — But Old Angel Midnight I love you, you love me, let ernest sink here, I'll snow him moon star lip kiss Out Save his breath ah vaun —

F is for

F

48 Mona Leisure

49 Tswit tswit the tsweep bird of tree in the roaring gulf day, hay blowing in the hay truck ho truck horizon roar of Orlandoar — Trazzz the truck goin by in seatree beachie roar — OAR! — take this I-see dream ferry, go ahead stare at grapefruit you forget how to smash medi-tate when you went richy you forget movies make you sit whittle sick stick whittlefool you'll never make it now except golden pencil hurl eternidad outa bird tswip lost in explorer moon — O grapefruit! orange wheee waving moss-old void Saturday ecstatic there-you-go world — O I know all now, think I'll shut up — You, folks, can hear the rest in ear

50 Old Angel Midnight the swan of heaven fell & flew cockmeek, Old Angel Midnigh the night onta twelve Year Tart with the long bing bong & the big ding dong, the boy on the sandbank blooming the moon, the sound wont let me sleep & since I found out time is silence Manjusri wont let me hear the swash of snow no mo in ole no po — O A M, Oh Om, the Old Midnacker snacker tired a twit twit twit the McTarty long true — the yentence peak peck slit slippymeek twang twall I'd heerd was flip the hand curse lead pencil in the shaky desk ah Ow HURT! — Tantapalii the silken tont retchy swan bent necky I wish I had enuf sense to swim as I hear, o lousy tired gal — One more! Choired arranged silence singers imbibing belly blum

51 Wreck the high charch chichipa & get firm juicy thebest thebest no other oil has ever heard such peanut squeeze — On top of which you yold yang midnockitwatter lying there in baid imagining casbah concepts from a highland fling moorish beach by moonlight medallion indicative spidergirls with sand legs waiting for the Non Christian cock, come O World Window Wowf & BARK! BARK! BARK for the girls of Tranatat — because by the time those two Mominuan monks with girls & boys in their matted hair pans sense wind in the flower the golden lord will turn the imbecile himself into slip paper — Or dog paper — or that pipe blend birds never peck because their bills are too hard — that window paper

52 Silence in my window now in the fullmoon of haiku which goes OO yellow continent in a birdbath, April full moon which rattles the goldroom little death chair that never will collapse even tho you sit 10

nymphet girls there on yr lap fall to the floor to cellars
of lust — and in any case O poet — O's of old world I
love yr greatness & anyways tho what kinda world we'd
have (Hi Missus Twazz) (O hullo Mr. Moon mock) a
world all poits? geen! try Mawln Bwano? rurt — The
old man is a moving plastic curtain whispering to find
his girls pare soundless possle, the lovers next door hid-
ing in back barn driveway the the the the the — Lottle
ma songing starty this is no time to listen to just but-
puff — shhh sez my Jetsun Yidam — Buddyo Ava Loki
T — in Ole Oaxaca we'll find the magic boatyard knifed
flame O wick, burn, or fall — The gossip among the
stars is that farledee who lit the moon end of dog turn
Turk Town Tenneduck was Kansased halfway to tripe
because the long thin Stick Men & the fat Slobs who ate
too much have their mouths sewed up, writers their
tongues yanked by hot irens, & Wolledockers of Old
Gallows England buried with the dust of ancient decap-
itated horses of old dust Japan in bowed head oblivion
that was meant for all things crumble & disappear
including (did you hear?) Lury Marsh, Goniff Tward,
Mic, Tokli Twa, Stabtalita Borotani, Parsh Tilyur, Cock,
Brrrocky ᴡᴊᴛᴌ ꟼᴓᴧ , & Tot.

53 Even from heaven now O ladies & gentlemen of
the fard world yr beloved angel dead are sighing sweet
memoried perfumed thoughts into yr ears to keep you
mindful that yr term on earth aint naught or for not, but
— bu yo bink the wick swans both twist to balls the
stasis hanging bathrobe — chairs crumble & get put

out on cleanup day, I saw one today I'd like to sit on the moon on & be a turnpage comedian continent cardown, tryna Satisfy Catholic girls from Harvard aint my pot a tea or plate a beans, I'se sorry oh son, lays & genmen, to the next Bardo (bardic?) (forgot) Tibetan (tiss top?) plot lins to find it Lama Lano lined the Turner Girl the mooma tannery where they say the bellrope sank the clank of pisspot grime the tanker that twirded for phantom Una southern Edward Papa river sod stashy slasheen girl Irish father iron Irish god's green earth & die there — either that, My Dame or pourquoi? — Bed wrinkled dinkled from too much sleets, mosser dear? Got shot charge Rebel joyous Georgian by witchcraft. Ah, & what lunchcart? The one with 69 year old daughters & 690 pound brothers & all the stars of Alex Manhole clear to Rubber O North Carolina Oklahoma Indian pips — urgh, & what else — The moon, this Friday evening she's already full & full & full on late afternoon board blue over trees & sandbanks — Dont mention his name! He will burn Buddha's babies in this house! He will hasten dust! Nothing but faith like Abraham believes in hallucinated true heart of dumb uneducated glimmering self 'cause the void is all illumined now & Milarepa had she-demons bouncing on his john because he loved red fires in his (fires in his?) — well, just red, Ned, & be sure to — to what? — bank the ikon — what Ikkon? The ikon silver cross that was almost buried with my brother — thank you brother — See you anon, my pat, my lemb, in Cielo soon's — soon's what? — soon's there's room in endless meaning

to accept another meaningless liar pushing pencil for to
die in happy breath so nobody could see

54   peep
                        peep the
                    bird tear the
                  sad bird drop heart
                the dawn has slung
              her aw arrow drape
            to sissyfoo & made eastpink
          dink the dimple solstice men
        crut and so the birds go ttleep
      and now bird number two three four five
    sixen seven and seven million of em den
  dead bens barking now the birds are yakking
& barking swinging Crack! Wow! Quiet! the
birds are making an awful racket in the Row
tweep ?   tswip !   creet !   clink !   crack !
ding dong the bell rope bird of break of day
            O k a y   b i r d s   q u i e t
                P l e a s e

                    you birds
                    robins
                      .black & blue birds
                    redbreasts & all
                      sisters, ———

                    my little parents
                    have the morning
                    by the golden balls

            And over there the sultan forgot

55   Ah old angel of midnight I cant hear myself think
for all your scur racket the lead in yr pencil on simple
asinine page so noisy what's a man gonna think of this
unless the rumble house black as snow horizon train
brings back all our favored dead from furnace & some-
body furnish — Ah car, a human directing his tatis-
matatagolre thru Holland to find the Dutch Imprimatur
to his Helem, the Helm & Cross of Charlemagne Euron
Irope that meant no more no less that Quebekois
Canoe (Kebokoa Kano) — Kak! But rumble will the
devil his will's unspoken, God wont truck helicopters
to peek-at-wisdom Vulture Queen, nor will the red dog
that glitters at the fish queen of my heart reach for kite
hook or Dahlenberg drent it any different for by
the great God Jesus I will not rest no wont rest till
Ferlinghetti's dog his day had does piss again on hy-
drant hydramatic stillness electrical ectroid where for
sure cats of the stripe so proud & vainty do vaunt for to
bring the final jumpmonkey home to Marpa's bird sing
— Ah translate me that — Cook! Dog echo in the sand-
bank valley Northport rumble Mahayana the diamond
Vajrayana path that was trod here long ago before those
houses jewel-graced the seaside hill, & for Krissakes no
sound at all comes in this window except those Wolf
Hourses got tamming bringing white & gray pearl
hearses thru the shoot rain to munner munner munner,
O fat eater in the drape son push yr belly back, the tape
worm — & worms to measure you, long tape — sod &
sand over yr bluenose disdain, Mrs America, the
Indian's Ya Ya Henna, the Indian Uprising known as the

Beat Generation, is going to eat rails & make tire sand-
wiches of every junkyard misty rust & all old heroes'
eyes in barley Soup of time — to be sopped with eye
sop — So carry on, escaper, jail's only made to flee —

The wush of trees on yonder eastern nabathaque
Latin Walden axe-haiku of hill where woodsman
Mahomet perceives will soon adown the morning drear
to pail the bringup well suspender farmer trap moon
so's cock go Bloody yurgle in the distance where
Timmy hides, flat, looking with his eyes for purr me —
O Angel, now is the time for all good men to come to
the aid of their party, & ah Angel dont paperparty me,
but make me honified in silken Honen honeyrubbéd
Oxen tongue of Cow Kiss, Ant Mat, silk girl ran, & all
the monkey-better-than secondary women of Sam Sarah
the Sang of Blood this earth, this tool, this fool, look
with your eyes, I'm tired of fooling O Angel bring it to
me THE MAGIC SOUND OF SILENCE broken by first-
bird's teepaleep ——

Good East! Hard to blow out! Sometimes! Darkness
in my final kip. This shot will send the gossip mongers
yarking back to Harvard frail slat, soft, full of gyzms in
slit lacéd hatreds for light is light O Lord, O Lord, I pray,
my Lord — Again! Once more! Ta ta ta ! Om

56 Ack, who gives a ruddy fuck about all this
American showoffy prose I'd like to know why Whane
meant horsefly & Brane something like, & why Owe's
Born is Awe's Dead, & all our intelligent handsome
Tedsy Boys go yearning after our pink pages & never

find & all the riots in Pixy Dilly & all the Traf on the Square, Elgar with his music doesn't impertaramount the rock of Murican roll? For strings? Air? O nonce, node, these babic yoiks, these Inds, these stupidities, these gem americans

57 TWO DAYS AGO, MARCH TWIP, 2059 (AXTONO) (WOW the twip of that carry-on I'll never fly another Yet to Souski that country wont feed me nothing but ersatz gatagatpataraze which is a kind (wow, the munsch) of farlidaltamanigalo the color of which, well, yr aunt Mary mighta told you but O the gossip in these other galaxies just too much my dear the rurn, the klen, the hoit, the noises of Flup. There was Onat Roren, Bob Torlignath the Crank, the Cranker of Hono-Machines, & the Bile Pister of the Falledern he was there be-sartifying all his meanies & the meannesses & told me I didnt have praper green in my pen gat — But he B.O. was alright, felt good, was glad because her time was late, & as for those publications up there that they turn out with all their bearded Trees extemporiating on the state of the talismanic oral pata —

I just got tired & retired but got involved in a long tat with Sinabad Talgamimargafonik Crud the interesting fool from the well located (in emerald waters) continent of Magic who told me there was a Sound recently developed by Shitteers that wd eventually require dog whistles hanging from breast teeth & bug micro bugs & long swarms of Milky Wayers vacationed over from Blue Curtain Country listening to the Country

Pard say: "The tanitat of this Omakorgeklid is infested with Imagery & therefore white as moon — but O my Thinkers never let it be said the sooth — " I couldnt listen to any more besides I had a deadline to meet & new flows to fii so came back to good old Tierra del Firma & had Princess my Tabtate, (solit) go eat another bont, which meant I only had 2 days to wait till today so rested up reading ancient texts & spent all night watching the sun on the moon the sinking mountain till all vanished & even MRS Stone made no comment but slept & that is my report to you today, my Dotggergsamtiian-idarstofgiviks

58   I just cant stand these people I teel you I dont know what I'm going to do about them, start my motor or fart my passage but you the way they carried on last night, *him,* with that dressy little deaful foosy on his lap the boom of busting chair & all that boommusic on the juke box & I dont know I wanted to call the police & get rid of this sandbag pineneedle Bodhi neighbor who is such ugly bearded dirty" ("nothing on earth or in any terrestrial sphere or in any Buddhalands Heaven or Mockswarm of Einsteinian & non-light Light can take hold my brothers & sisters & cousins because it is only the wisdom of manifested epiphany & the compassion of goodbye" —) (as soon as I can find a bully club & bang a hole in imaginary fence I tell you this will be the last time the window's with redlegged devils & stone blue eyes —) (Kunfii, garayen, hallo Kiyan, fitiguwi, katapatafataja, silya, kitipuwee, senlou, saint loup,

coish, karan) (or vaunt the moidners the Villa Viva
Pancho baby Mexico City sorefoot Juarez old hotel
wino El Paso march picking up six thousand partisans
to vest the peon with his land coat so that years later
Rivera murals shine by army teahead trumpet in Ole
Texcoco) "there'll come a day when that yurn I'll have
to astabing the zemble the cartifacartilage I wont have
another moment of — Dry up, dry up, moist earth, dry
up, dust ball, dutball moon is sick of leering at your
inadmissable sorrow because it has no twat to to tie
onto't — And we the fooly libs that think ah music air-
plane & all ye screaming birds of falsedawn let the
ephemera existence wait at yr side with you for end
to't — No other teaching hear & hear tell & what of
that the sound who wants to hear — Go fetch the gar-
dles & make open the corridors of your Bright Room
mind the Lord is coming he's all white & gold, he's a
pink white angel in a black room by a blue window & a
yellow candleflame with golden (hurt) wings the color
of all thingness, the swarming dove, there! See it! He
stands at yr non-side sides the waterbaby by the baby
shroud, the honeyfall, the bliss blessed to be believed,
the final pollitabimackatatanabala (fine as fine can be)
(Ah Ah) (HO HO) leap & dance it's saved! the nerve of
that man ! foru ! mon ti kitaya ! patakatafataya — perk !
prick ! prick ears I mean you think I let pollute window
liars? Oh God, stop it —

When God snaps his Finger of Gold & suspenders
too the world will wake in the well looking at the dark

star — this silvery desert full of gophers rattlesnake tracks & sobbing moons of Chihuahuan splendor I'll buy, tho, till that Babe of the Honied Fall is at my side again for nothing, nothing, nothing, absolutely power- fully lightly emptily goldenly eternally nothing ever hap- pened & this I bring to you from grass i the sun (to tell of it, the cock in card the soft & mixup pushing bardahl Drutchen cant & dent of it I wount hav it, ht Anyway) (seurain) (sunrin) (booya) J'm'enva arretez ! Fo.

59 Aw rust rust rust rust die die die pipe pipe ash ash die die ding dong ding ding ding rust cob die pipe ass rust die words — I'd as rather be permiganted in Rusty's moonlight Rork as be perdirated in this bile arta panataler where ack the orshy rosh crowshes my tired idiot hand O Lawd I is coming to you's soon's you's ready's as can readies be Mazatlan heroes point out Mexicos & all ye rhythmic bay fishermen dont hang fiish eye soppy in my Ramadam givecigarette Sop of Arab Squat — the Berber types that hang fardels on their woman back wd as lief Erick some son with blady matter I guess as whup a mule in singsong pathetic mulejump field by quiet fluff smoke North Carolina (near Weldon) (Railroad Bridge) Roanoke Millionaire High-Ridge hi-party Hi-Fi milliondollar findriver skinfish Rod Tong Apple Finder John Sun Ford goodby Paw mule America Song —

60 Arguing about mudpies in the hot spring sun karu, myota the Japanese   who wrote of   was always concerned about his poison oak hut when they came bringing him early dogwood buds with a bleached rock & the trinity of rocks & yak of blackbird pearbranch jumping & the Umpteen yumping erse Norway Man of N'o'r'm'a'n'd'i'a (who repaired houses?) (who made new moons bider) (brighter) (?) (bider) of time the bider the cross in his tomb worm & the King on his epistaff stone tomb port of north — Oh — All ties in you see like fish pier respect.

Fish spear shook? — shook aimed & breton rocked —

O but just as long as sun shines like this in yellow airplane on the pebble Beach sky & pear yump yak blossoms (up north) — & as long as red hydrants & post chaises — (gossip?) (Well it's a quiet moment but methinks the sons of the world & daughters thereof as wellus wolves & loups will be perfectly containted as long as they stay away from Ehrlich's dyemill blue-worms which are et by OObaltory golbords & clover'ed & clobbered by mind's no-nature essence & as soon as they ask for an explanation say "What? buds in blue new sky?"

Dream for Muggy Mojump the quiet cloud.

61 Kertion Kerdion Keryon Kerson cherson & Who else in this ugly old Russia hechavel helps me in this business recordin sounds of universe midnight? but not a single damn dull fool podium hear it attestify that the selickman was a poet who decided to say:

I am a poet

&

here is my poem
Watch how fancy I write
Skeletons of Compassion dusting
in the distant heavens' infinity
while fat old burbles rememberem

well

here

on high hark — high hart —
world — diepork —

Over & above of which it was down in Charleston
West Virginny one time my Pa in white shirt & un-
shaved shot a man in a poolroom fight — they chased
him acrosst the Kanowa in a Kanoea (idiot) & got him
down by the bayin hope dogs in that country where
Old Angel Mama Midnight will lean her happy head &
hungry eyes on pillows of Old in the high falutin poem
of Heaven where little white house it waitin for all you
black sufferers so's dandy'll say "Twas all writ & no
more to say, the Vow of Gold is Done" & all yet young
kids wanta know what a man do when he golden baby
post up there he completes the vow matures the Karma
returns the Kitkat Clowns the Crown Thorns the Flap
and dad blasts him happiness forever, because you'll
see, in not too many years now, yr hope & grace-waves
werent jivin ya, all's taken care of behind these suffer-
ing trees & inside these suffering bees & wont nobody
harsh ya but say kind star roof words & bring white

cloth to your laundryboy basket (clean as dinosaur
teeth) & you'll know the — sore yah he was sore but he
said Bust me one on the jaw, I got the running eyes —
With or without sugar — The Cat in the Con-Cord
   Lord, you presumptuous goodgiver, thanks, & go
tell everybody you Vowin hardass sonsumbitchcs —
(hold clasp hand TaTaTa) — Aye Bodhidharma

62   Tapistry the second writer
       in the novel island bearded
       scared wont use words saves
       he go's & hungerers of wood
       from boom in the Spain Jail
          hand on knees

       To go cross cemetery America
       highwire ratcroak dumpslaver
       moogow silo sillwindow rat
       wait moon shine on tin
       all the little inner outer sin

          peek at the bird
             tree, remember
          it again, the
       hoosegow goddam cuban
          Killer who moidners
             turtles, traps em cock
             in the nigh & never
             draps a wear

All day nervous wonderin what to do shoe in my arm-
chair innesfoo that was writ in Akashia I'm just hearin
what my head said & it's mighty repetitiousness

63   The black ants that roosted in my tree all winter
long have just emerged to meet an army of enemy ants
(same breed) & a big war is now taking place, I just
looked with my brakemans lamp (by sunlight) (brake
the day sun) warriors are biting each other's sensitive
rear humps & killing each other with more intelligence
about murder than my boot knows — I squashed one
wounded warrior whose poor right front armorer was
missing & he just croualtad coupled there, I hated to
see him suffer & he was open (ow) for attack too, bit
safe a mo on a flat rock used for lady's flagstones in the
pink tea world which ignores ant Wars & doesnt know
that when the first space ship lands on the planet
Amtasagrak (really Katapatafaya in other galuxies) the
ship will immediately be swarmed over by black ants,
even the window obscured, they'll have to turn their X-
Roentgen Gun Ray on it to see & what they'll see'll
make em wish Von Braun had stayed in brown ger-
many: one sextillion sextillion idiot insect fiends a foot
deep eating one another endlessly the top ones scuf-
fling, the next layer dead & being nibbled, the next
layer belly to belly cant move from the weight, & the
bottom layer suffocated at last — & the lady ants have
wings & fly to little tiny planets that hang six feet above
the moiling black shiny ant sea, where they hatch, push
the grownup kids off (into the Mess) & die Sighing for

Paradise O ye singers of War & Glory

After seeing a thing like this who wd dare not ask for enlightenment everywhere? Who will deny ant war with me?

Meanwhile in my yard the triumphant winning warrior ant stands over his defeated dying brother & you see his little antled helmet waving in the glorious breeze like How Ta Ra the trumpets of Harfleur & (you know what I was going to say there — hm —) no compassion in these little febrile finicular skeleton — O Ant Soup !

64 O Escapade escape me never I lied I lied I lied I'll never escape ex cape — of Spaign — God'll ever me allow to leave this hurt of ant scene until I lissen to his words & wave & point by saucer moon & antlered antennae &

weird roofwash & weirder cross windows, the black clock by the white clock in the city's creamy tenement while one silk stocking waves to gossip the lady's lost leg & there's a slip by a pair of paints waving in the moon breeze as well as a sheet which however has no blaind stain of blood, only the one silk stocking — & there's panties, littleboy pants, handkerchiefs, towels & many cursed faint bigscrew'd oratan furykula yaink antavyazers, with black hooks, sword spaces, windows the bottoms falling out & the moon a crink in its upper neck which is really its back (Ah)

65 That grassy yocker pocking up yonder

66   Tonight the full apogee May moon will out, early with a jaundiced tint, & pop angels all over my rooftop along with Devas sprinkling flowers, pilgrims dropping turds & sweet nemanucalar nameless railroad trains from heaven with omnipotent youths bearing monkey women that will stomp through the stage waiting for the moment when by pinching myself I prove that a thought is like a touch, unless someone sicks a hot iron in my heart or heaps up Evil Karma like tit and tat the pile of that and pulls my mother out her bed to slay her before my damning dying human eyes and I break my head on heads — Everytime you throw a rock at a cat from your glass house you heap upon yourself the automatic Stanley Gould winter so dark of death after death, & growing old, because lady those ashcans'll bite you back & be cold too, and your son will never rest in the imperturbable knowledge that what he thinks he thinks as well as what he does he thinks as well as what he feels he thinks as well as future that.

Future that my damn old sword cutter Paison Pasha Lost the Preakness again.

Tonight the moon shall witness angels trooping at the baby's window where inside he gurgles in his pewk looking with mewling eyes for babyside waterfall lambikin hillside the day the little arab shepherd boy hugged the babylamb to heart while the mother bleeted at his bay heel — And so Joe the sillicks killit no not — Shhhhoww graaa — wing & car-start — The angels devas monsters asuras Devadattas Vedantas McLaughlins Stones will hue & hurl in hell if they don't love the lamb the lamb the lam of hell lambchop. Why did Scott Fitzgerald keep a notebook? Such a marvelous notebook.

67   Komi denera ness pata sutyamp anda wanda vesnoki shadakiroo paryoumemga sikarem nora sarkadium baron roy kellegiam myorki ayastuna haidanseetzel ampho andiam yerka yama chelmsford alya bonneavance koroom cemada versel

(The 26th Annual concert of The Armenian Convention)

Editor's Note:

Sections 1-49 of *Old Angel Midnight* were first published in *Big Table*, Spring 1959. Sections 50-67 were published in *Evergreen Review*, August/September 1964. Sections 50 & 51 appeared as "More *Old Angel Midnight*" in *New Directions in Prose & Poetry* No. 17 (1961). And in 1992 John Sampas found "A Piece of *Old Angel Midnight*" amongst Jack Kerouac's papers.   D.A.

More *Old Angel Midnight*

Old Angel Midnight the swan of heaven fell
        and flew cockmeek
Old Angel Midnigh the night onta twelve
        Year Tart with the long bing bong
        and the big ding dong
The boy on the sandbank blooming the moon,
The sound won't let me sleep and since I
        found out time is silence Manjusri won't
        let me hear the swash of snow no mo
        in ole no po
O A M
Oh O M
Tho old Midnacker snacker tired a twit twit twit
        the Mc Tarty long true
The yentence peak peck slit slippymeek twang
        twall I'd heerd was flip the hand curse
        lead pencil in the shaky desk

Ah ow HURT!

Tantapalii the silken tont retchy swan
      bent necky I wish I had enuf sense to swim
      as I hear

O lousy tired gal

One more!

Choired arranged silence singers imbibing
      belly blum

Wreck the high charch chichipa and get firm
      juicy thebest thebest no other oil
      has ever heard such peanut squeeze

On top of which you yold yang midnockitwatter
      lying there in baid imagining casbah concepts
      from a highland fling moorish beach
      by moonlight medallion indicative spidergirls
      with sand legs waiting for the non-Christian
      cock, come O World window Wowf

& BARK!

  BARK!

  BARK for the girls of Tranatat

Because by the time those two Mominuan monks
      with girls & boys in their matted hair pans
      sense wind in the flower the golden lord will
      turn the imbecile himself into slip paper

Or dog paper

Or that pipe blend birds never peck because
      their bills are too hard

That window paper.

Tool the tirlishes down, mejems seemst Ide time Saturday or Nunday, one O shot shick razor cut and meating this is the sharp blade of grass cuts the innocent 'and when lambs bray — yay — and all the tapeboos & topatoos go cruing in Pakis Tanny the Loola Place where hides are bared, haired, & mared — or slunked with one axe head meat smap

That story you'se expectin O Brer Rabmollasoses you old Taird Tender Grant Cigared you at Appo ten thousand or more dead — daid — Eyes of Ray Charles see Me here realize O Holy